Deep Thoughts of the Book Worm Daily Planner.

Activinotes

Activinotes

DAILY JOURNALS, PLANNERS, NOTEBOOKS AND OTHER BLANK BOOKS

A Daily Planner

Date :

Time:	Activity

THOUGHTS FOR THE DAY

COMMENTS:

A Daily Planner

Date:

Time:	Activity

THOUGHTS FOR THE DAY

COMMENTS:

A Daily Planner

Date :

Time:	Activity

THOUGHTS FOR THE DAY

COMMENTS:

A Daily Planner

Date:	

Time:	Activity

THOUGHTS FOR THE DAY

COMMENTS:

A Daily Planner

Date :

Time:	Activity

THOUGHTS FOR THE DAY

COMMENTS:

A Daily Planner

Date:

Time:	Activity

THOUGHTS FOR THE DAY

COMMENTS:

A Daily Planner

Date :

Time:	Activity

THOUGHTS FOR THE DAY

COMMENTS:

A Daily Planner

Date:

Time:	Activity

THOUGHTS FOR THE DAY

COMMENTS:

A Daily Planner

Date :

Time:	Activity

THOUGHTS FOR THE DAY

COMMENTS:

A Daily Planner

Date:

Time:	Activity

THOUGHTS FOR THE DAY

COMMENTS:

A Daily Planner

Date:

Time:	Activity

THOUGHTS FOR THE DAY

COMMENTS:

A Daily Planner

Date:

Time:	Activity

THOUGHTS FOR THE DAY

COMMENTS:

A Daily Planner

Date :

Time:	Activity

THOUGHTS FOR THE DAY

COMMENTS:

A Daily Planner

Date :

Time:	Activity

THOUGHTS FOR THE DAY

COMMENTS:

A Daily Planner

Date :

Time:	Activity

THOUGHTS FOR THE DAY

COMMENTS:

A Daily Planner

Date :

Time:	Activity

THOUGHTS FOR THE DAY

COMMENTS:

A Daily Planner

Date :

Time:	Activity

THOUGHTS FOR THE DAY

COMMENTS:

A Daily Planner

Date:

Time:	Activity

THOUGHTS FOR THE DAY

COMMENTS:

A Daily Planner

Date:

Time:	Activity

THOUGHTS FOR THE DAY

COMMENTS:

A Daily Planner

Date:

Time:	Activity

THOUGHTS FOR THE DAY

COMMENTS:

A Daily Planner

Date :

Time:	Activity

THOUGHTS FOR THE DAY

COMMENTS:

A Daily Planner

Date:

Time:	Activity

THOUGHTS FOR THE DAY

COMMENTS:

A Daily Planner

Date :

Time:	Activity

THOUGHTS FOR THE DAY

COMMENTS:

A Daily Planner

Date :

Time:	Activity

THOUGHTS FOR THE DAY

COMMENTS:

A Daily Planner

Date:

Time:	Activity

THOUGHTS FOR THE DAY

COMMENTS:

A Daily Planner

Date:

Time:	Activity

THOUGHTS FOR THE DAY

COMMENTS:

A Daily Planner

Date :

Time:	Activity

THOUGHTS FOR THE DAY

COMMENTS:

A Daily Planner

Date:

Time:	Activity

THOUGHTS FOR THE DAY

COMMENTS:

A Daily Planner

Date :

Time:	Activity

THOUGHTS FOR THE DAY

COMMENTS:

A Daily Planner

Date:

Time:	Activity

THOUGHTS FOR THE DAY

COMMENTS:

A Daily Planner

Date :

Time:	Activity

THOUGHTS FOR THE DAY

COMMENTS:

A Daily Planner

Date:

Time:	Activity

THOUGHTS FOR THE DAY

COMMENTS:

A Daily Planner

Date:

Time:	Activity

THOUGHTS FOR THE DAY

COMMENTS:

A Daily Planner

Date:

Time:	Activity

THOUGHTS FOR THE DAY

COMMENTS:

A Daily Planner

Date :

Time:	Activity

THOUGHTS FOR THE DAY

COMMENTS:

A Daily Planner

Date :

Time:	Activity

THOUGHTS FOR THE DAY

COMMENTS:

A Daily Planner

Date:

Time:	Activity

THOUGHTS FOR THE DAY

COMMENTS:

A Daily Planner

Date:

Time:	Activity

THOUGHTS FOR THE DAY

COMMENTS:

A Daily Planner

Date :

Time:	Activity

THOUGHTS FOR THE DAY

COMMENTS:

A Daily Planner

Date:

Time:	Activity

THOUGHTS FOR THE DAY

COMMENTS:

A Daily Planner

Date:

Time:	Activity

THOUGHTS FOR THE DAY

COMMENTS:

A Daily Planner

Date:	

Time:	Activity

THOUGHTS FOR THE DAY

COMMENTS:

A Daily Planner

Date :

Time:	Activity

THOUGHTS FOR THE DAY

COMMENTS:

A Daily Planner

Date:

Time:	Activity

THOUGHTS FOR THE DAY

COMMENTS:

A Daily Planner

Date:

Time:	Activity

THOUGHTS FOR THE DAY

COMMENTS:

A Daily Planner

Date :

Time:	Activity

THOUGHTS FOR THE DAY

COMMENTS:

A Daily Planner

Date :

Time:	Activity

THOUGHTS FOR THE DAY

COMMENTS:

A Daily Planner

Date :

Time:	Activity

THOUGHTS FOR THE DAY

COMMENTS:

A Daily Planner

Date :

Time:	Activity

THOUGHTS FOR THE DAY

COMMENTS:

A Daily Planner

Date:

Time:	Activity

THOUGHTS FOR THE DAY

COMMENTS:

A Daily Planner

Date :

Time:	Activity

THOUGHTS FOR THE DAY

COMMENTS:

A Daily Planner

Date:

Time:	Activity

THOUGHTS FOR THE DAY

COMMENTS:

A Daily Planner

Date:

Time:	Activity

THOUGHTS FOR THE DAY

COMMENTS:

A Daily Planner

Date :

Time:	**Activity**

THOUGHTS FOR THE DAY

COMMENTS:

A Daily Planner

Date :

Time:	Activity

THOUGHTS FOR THE DAY

COMMENTS:

A Daily Planner

Date:

Time:	Activity

THOUGHTS FOR THE DAY

COMMENTS:

A Daily Planner

Date :

Time:	Activity

THOUGHTS FOR THE DAY

COMMENTS:

A Daily Planner

Date :

Time:	Activity

THOUGHTS FOR THE DAY

COMMENTS:

A Daily Planner

Date :

Time:	Activity

THOUGHTS FOR THE DAY

COMMENTS:

A Daily Planner

Date:

Time:	Activity

THOUGHTS FOR THE DAY

COMMENTS:

A Daily Planner

Date:

Time:	Activity

THOUGHTS FOR THE DAY

COMMENTS:

A Daily Planner

Date:

Time:	Activity

THOUGHTS FOR THE DAY

COMMENTS:

A Daily Planner

Date :

Time:	Activity

THOUGHTS FOR THE DAY

COMMENTS:

A Daily Planner

Date:

Time:	Activity

THOUGHTS FOR THE DAY

COMMENTS:

A Daily Planner

Date:

Time:	Activity

THOUGHTS FOR THE DAY

COMMENTS:

A Daily Planner

Date:

Time:	Activity

THOUGHTS FOR THE DAY

COMMENTS:

A Daily Planner

Date :

Time:	Activity

THOUGHTS FOR THE DAY

COMMENTS:

A Daily Planner

Date:

Time:	Activity

THOUGHTS FOR THE DAY

COMMENTS:

A Daily Planner

Date :	

Time:	Activity

THOUGHTS FOR THE DAY

COMMENTS:

A Daily Planner

Date :

Time:	Activity

THOUGHTS FOR THE DAY

COMMENTS:

A Daily Planner

Date:	

Time:	Activity

THOUGHTS FOR THE DAY

COMMENTS:

A Daily Planner

Date :

Time:	Activity

THOUGHTS FOR THE DAY

COMMENTS:

A Daily Planner

Date:

Time:	Activity

THOUGHTS FOR THE DAY

COMMENTS:

A Daily Planner

Date:

Time:	Activity

THOUGHTS FOR THE DAY

COMMENTS:

A Daily Planner

Date :

Time:	Activity

THOUGHTS FOR THE DAY

COMMENTS:

A Daily Planner

Date:

Time:	Activity

THOUGHTS FOR THE DAY

COMMENTS:

A Daily Planner

Date:

Time:	Activity

THOUGHTS FOR THE DAY

COMMENTS:

A Daily Planner

Date :

Time:	Activity

THOUGHTS FOR THE DAY

COMMENTS:

A Daily Planner

Date:

Time:	Activity

THOUGHTS FOR THE DAY

COMMENTS:

A Daily Planner

Date:

Time:	Activity

THOUGHTS FOR THE DAY

COMMENTS:

A Daily Planner

Date :

Time:	Activity

THOUGHTS FOR THE DAY

COMMENTS:

A Daily Planner

Date:

Time:	Activity

THOUGHTS FOR THE DAY

COMMENTS:

A Daily Planner

Date :

Time:	Activity

THOUGHTS FOR THE DAY

COMMENTS:

A Daily Planner

Date :

Time:	Activity

THOUGHTS FOR THE DAY

COMMENTS:

A Daily Planner

Date :

Time:	Activity

THOUGHTS FOR THE DAY

COMMENTS:

A Daily Planner

Date:

Time:	Activity

THOUGHTS FOR THE DAY

COMMENTS:

A Daily Planner

Date:

Time:	**Activity**

THOUGHTS FOR THE DAY

COMMENTS:

A Daily Planner

Date :

Time:	Activity

THOUGHTS FOR THE DAY

COMMENTS:

A Daily Planner

Date:

Time:	Activity

THOUGHTS FOR THE DAY

COMMENTS:

A Daily Planner

Date:	

Time:	Activity

THOUGHTS FOR THE DAY

COMMENTS:

A Daily Planner

Date:	

Time:	Activity

THOUGHTS FOR THE DAY

COMMENTS:

A Daily Planner

Date:

Time:	Activity

Thoughts for the Day

COMMENTS:

A Daily Planner

Date:

Time:	Activity

THOUGHTS FOR THE DAY

COMMENTS:

A Daily Planner

Date:

Time:	Activity

THOUGHTS FOR THE DAY

COMMENTS:

A Daily Planner

Date:

Time:	Activity

THOUGHTS FOR THE DAY

COMMENTS:

A Daily Planner

Date :

Time:	Activity

THOUGHTS FOR THE DAY

COMMENTS:

A Daily Planner

Date:	

Time:	Activity

THOUGHTS FOR THE DAY

COMMENTS:

A Daily Planner

Date:

Time:	Activity

THOUGHTS FOR THE DAY

COMMENTS:

A Daily Planner

Date:

Time:	Activity

THOUGHTS FOR THE DAY

COMMENTS:

A Daily Planner

Date:

Time:	Activity

THOUGHTS FOR THE DAY

COMMENTS:

A Daily Planner

Date:

Time:	Activity

THOUGHTS FOR THE DAY

COMMENTS:

A Daily Planner

Date:

Time:	Activity

THOUGHTS FOR THE DAY

COMMENTS:

A Daily Planner

Date:

Time:	Activity

THOUGHTS FOR THE DAY

COMMENTS:

A Daily Planner

Date:

Time:	Activity

THOUGHTS FOR THE DAY

COMMENTS:

www.ingramcontent.com/pod-product-compliance
Lightning Source LLC
Chambersburg PA
CBHW080736250626
47170CB00010B/2853